FRANK MEADOW SUTCLIFFE

Hon F.R.P.S

Whitby and its people as seen by one of the founders of the naturalistic movement in photography.

A third selection of his work compiled by Michael Shaw.

The Sutcliffe Gallery,
1 Flowergate,
Whitby, North Yorkshire,
YO21 3BA, England.

First Published 1990

Published and © 1990 by:

The Sutcliffe Gallery
1 Flowergate, Whitby, North Yorkshire, YO21 3BA,
England.   Tel: (0947) 602239

By agreement with Whitby Literary & Philosophical Society

Photographic printing:	Graeme Porter, Warrens Photolabs, Leeds
Photographic finishing:	Colin Roberts, Warrens Photolabs, Leeds
Scanning & Origination:	Reprotech Studio, York
Typesetting:	The House of Type, Guisborough
Duotone printing:	Studio Print, Guisborough
Book binding:	John Joyce & Son, Gateshead
Additional research:	Sue Boyes, Sutcliffe Gallery, Whitby

ISBN Numbers
Hard Cover Limited Edition 0 9503175 7 8
Soft Cover General Edition 0 9503175 6 X

Front cover photograph:
Frank Meadow Sutcliffe taken by his daughter Irene.

INTRODUCTION

The world has seen an almost bewildering rate of change throughout this century and certainly since we published the first selection of Frank Meadow Sutcliffe's work in 1974 it has become a perceptively smaller place. Amongst other things, satellite television enables instant, live images from the latest trouble spot − no matter how distant, to create a greater or lesser impact on our senses. Unless they have some outstanding quality these images are quickly driven out of our minds by superseding footage. Why then do some photographs have an enduring attraction even though produced using − by today's standards − extremely 'low-tech' equipment and materials?

Sutcliffe's work has just such an appeal. Could it be that the philosophy behind the photograph is infinitely more important than the technology used in its taking? Frank Sutcliffe, writing in the magazine 'Photography' of 31st May 1894 has this to say about the difficulties of learning how to take a photograph:

> "If this problem is addressed to a dealer in apparatus, the answer is, 'Oh, dear no, all you require is one of our cameras, and the rest is as easy as A B C,' not that A B C was easy to any of us to learn.

> If addressed to a young photographer, the answer will be, 'No, it is easy enough until you come to the toning, then your troubles begin; most of the stuff they sell for toning is of no use,' &c., &c.

> But if an old photographer is addressed, he will reply that 'anyone who can *see* can photograph.' In time it will dawn on the worker as he grows older that his sight *is* improving, that many things which he had overlooked are making themselves visible, and he will then try to cultivate his sight, a thing he thought unnecessary before.

> It is so easy to work with the eyes shut in a blindfold fashion, firing off at anything and everything in the hope that the camera may hit off something worth looking at now and then.

> The student in search of the picturesque will soon find that the beauty of a subject depends more on the condition under which it is seen than the material of which it is composed, and often the less material there is the better the chance of success."

Or this, later in the same article:

> "... for people have been taught to look upon the camera as an instrument wherewith the most elaborate subjects can be reproduced down to the most microscopic atom; but who is going to carry away in their mind's eye a memory picture of these wonderful photographs − take a view of a house for instance, where every brick stands out clearly, who can carry away all these bricks in his mind? Yet a picture of this very house, taken when, maybe, no bricks were visible, might so please the spectator that the impression made on his brain might charm for months to come."

At the time of publishing our previous books Michael Hiley's monograph on Sutcliffe (now unfortunately out of print) was readily available and we thought it unnecessary to include a great deal of biographic information, preferring instead to devote as much space as possible to the pictures themselves.

Such details we are still keeping to a minimum, favouring a more penetrating look at the man's mind than a recital of dates and places.

Nevertheless, for those who wish to have a more factual account of his life: Frank Meadow Sutcliffe was born on 6th October 1853 at Headingley, Leeds, the son of Thomas Sutcliffe, member of 'The Institute of Painters in Water Colours' who was equally at home working in oil colours, lithography, etching and photography. He saw a great future in the latter and owned what was probably the first camera in Leeds. Charles Noel Armfield, writing on Thomas Sutcliffe in 'Sun Artists' magazine, July 1891 thought that perhaps his greatest power was as an 'artistic analyst'.

As a teenager Frank was already busy mastering the difficulties of the wet-plate process of photography and taking photographs of his friends and neighbours.

In 1870 the Sutcliffe family moved to Whitby where they had spent their summer holidays since Frank's childhood. On 12th December the following year Thomas died at the age of forty three. He had suggested before his death that Frank should take up photography as a profession and as he was now the breadwinner for the family Frank began to develop his hobby into a livelihood.

After a short and abortive attempt to establish a portrait business in Tunbridge Wells he returned to Whitby in 1875 and set up a small studio in Waterloo Yard in what had been a jet workshop.

Shortly before setting up this studio he had married a Whitby girl called Eliza Duck.

Whitby was, and is, a holiday town with a short season and long winters. Whilst his business prospered during the hectic holiday periods, there was often not sufficient work during the rest of the year and his creative genius prompted him to photograph the wealth of subject matter which was around him. Over the succeeding years he gradually produced the photographs by which we know him today.

In 1894 he opened a new studio at 25, Skinner Street. These were much larger premises, and judging from contemporary reports were well fitted out and equipped, both photographically and for the convenience of his clients.

Sutcliffe retired from photography in 1922 to be able to devote more time to Whitby museum of which he became curator in 1923. He held this position until shortly before his death in 1941 at the age of 87.

Sutcliffe was closely connected with the London Salon and 'The Linked Ring', a loose association of pictorial photographers who wished to be free of the tradition of formalised photography popular during that period. His work did much to advance the status of photography as an art and partly for this reason he was elected an Honorary Fellow of the Royal Photographic society in 1935 – the highest photographic distinction attainable in this country.

The personality of Frank Sutcliffe has never really emerged from accounts given to me by people who reputedly knew him well – probably due to the 'staggered' time periods involved. His own writings do however, seem to reveal far more of the person. I am indebted to Michael Hiley, who, during the research he carried out for his book on Sutcliffe published by Gordon Fraser, London in 1974 brought to light the following excerpt from The Photographic News magazine of November 16th 1888.

The Camera Club in London had just mounted their first 'One Man Exhibition' – this devoted to the work of Frank Meadow Sutcliffe then thirty five years old. It appears that he had been asked by the editor of the magazine to contribute a potted autobiography. It reads as follows:

"I am very pleased to hear that you consider the exhibition such a success. Pray don't apologise for asking questions; it is quite a pleasant relief to turn from water-rate questions, income-tax, house-duty, &c. which are bothering the life out of me to answer them.

1. In answer to your question about skies, we do not prepare collodion negatives requiring separate printings. I should if I had time, and patience, to do so.

2. None of the photographs are combinations of figure or foreground with painted backgrounds, except one or two heads and one three-quarter figure, which were taken in the studio, and 'The Old Whaler's Head'.

I am very sorry that I have not a portrait of myself. I was once taken on the sands on glass by a touting photographer, along with my wife, but she won't part with it. I was also taken when a boy at school. I am afraid I cannot describe myself very well. A nephew of mine says I am very like Julius Caesar, but I am not sufficiently well read in Roman history to know whether he had red hair or not. An old woman once told me I looked like a linen-draper, because I had long arms and could reach things off the shelves. You ask for a note or two of my eventful career. Well, I was born by the roadside. My father was a landscape painter, member of the Institute of Painters in Water-Colours. I used to roam about hill and dale with him, eating blackberries, climbing trees, tickling trout, catching butterflies, bird-nesting, gathering wild flowers, till I was fourteen, when some one said it was time I was doing something: so I was sent to a brewery in Leeds to learn to be a clerk. But the smoke and noise were too much for me. On the top of a bookshelf I found a book, "On Photography, Lake Price". I wondered why the 'lake' price for a book should be different from that charged elsewhere. I took it down to see. My father who saw me, said: 'I think you'll have to try photography.' You see my mother had told me from earliest infancy that she would have me smothered like the Princes in the Tower if I showed any inclination for being an artist. She thought all artists little better than lunatics. For years I used to dream that a man was coming to smother me. My sleeping-place was Bolton Castle, and for years I dreamed that I had to get up and run away down the Castle steps.

My father found me an old camera, and made part of an out-house into a dark room. I then used to amuse myself with photographing the neighbours, &c.

When I was seventeen my father died. He got caught by the tide on the rocks while painting, not far from here. This brought on heart disease. A friend of mine, who knew Mr. Frith, got him to give me some work among the abbeys &c., in Yorkshire; but the price paid did not cover my expenses in having to wait for fine weather – abbeys, &c., wanting the sun, of course. I had before this had a summer on the lakes, photographing for a lot of friends of my father's who had houses at Derwent, Ullswater, and Coniston. I then decided to take a situation in a photographer's studio. I waited for three years, but the much-looked-for place never came.

I then thought I would build a studio for myself, and decided on Tunbridge Wells as the best place. Having read so much from the pen of H.P. Robinson about charging well for your work, I, in my innocence, thought the photographers there would charge at least £4 a dozen for carte portraits. I spent some £600 on studio – all I had; was there nearly two years; had only fifty sitters; sold all up to pay increasing debts; came back here; turned a jet-shop into a studio; am here still, taking portraits of babies and twins, and groups of young children, and old maids.

Sometimes I get out with my camera before breakfast. If I venture out in the daytime I am sure to meet a fond parent who is bringing little Johnnie to be taken again, as his grandmother (who is nearly blind) thinks he is laughing too much. How I envy that Italian photographer who can afford to refuse to take all sitters but those he thinks will make good pictures.

You asked for description of incidents connected with the photographs. Am afraid I can't send you any. I have just had all the life knocked out of me. A man, one of the North-Eastern Railway Company's men, has just been here. Said he had a son who wished to become a photographer. I asked if the lad was strong. His father replied that he was not, but thought that did not matter. In fact, he said his son was subject to fits. He had been to sea, but had had a fit one day, when up aloft. Had fallen down on the deck and broken his arm and thigh. Had had to leave sea, and had been fit for nothing ever since; so he had come to see if I could make a 'likeness-taker' of him. What is the use of anything after that?

A fisherman appearing on one of the photographs exhibited asked me how old I thought the three of them were. I did not know. He replied, nigh on 300 years; but I found he counted the age of his coble as well, when speaking of the age of his partner and himself.

By the way, from a letter I had this morning, a lady in London thinks I am personally conducting my show, for she writes to know if I can take her photograph at the exhibition on Friday or Saturday."

With our lightweight, compact cameras it is easy to forget the physical tribulations endured by these early photographers − spelled out in no uncertain manner in the following article by Sutcliffe in 'The Amateur Photographer' magazine of 30th March 1900.

"I have been taking photographs with an old camera for twenty-five years. A year ago I started in with a new camera. I had got pretty well tired of taking photographs with the old camera. The old camera, too, had like its owner, got tired. The screws which held it together had got tired of 'biting', they were continually 'leaving go' either the front or the back of the camera; either the weight of the dark slide behind, or the weight of the lens before, was like the last straw on the camel's back, just as the weight of the camera and its six dark slides often felt like the last straw on my back. I used to fill the slides with plates and go out into the country in search of the picturesque, but before I had got clear of the town I had forgotten my quest altogether, for the camera began to get so heavy that the picturesque was forgotten, and my thoughts were entirely confined to the burden on my back, and the weights I carried in either hand. Yet, as an Englishman, I did not like to feel beaten, so I used to trudge on, the camera getting heavier all the way, till at last a rest was imperative. If there happened to be a picture near the resting spot, well and good; if not I either went on or back, as the spirit moved me."

On the subject of studio portrait photography Sutcliffe has said that he was 'nothing special'. Yet a significant part of his writings were devoted to this theme. Our picture of him today is strongly influenced by the photographs for which he has become famous − those reproduced in this book are typical. It is easy to forget that it was mainly from commissioned portrait work that he made his living ...

"By noting the pattern on the carpet it is easy to snap the babe as it crawls near the right spot. By this means focusing is not needed, whereas if the baby is put into a chair, the picture, no matter how sharp, is an absurd one, for no mother in her senses would ever put a young baby into a chair and leave it there; she would be sure to put in on the floor where it would be safe."

This from The Amateur Photographer magazine of August 25, 1899 on the problems of focusing in the studio.

It is snippets like the following that illustrate the frustrations felt by early photographers when wrestling with their equipment:

"Every portrait photographer knows too well that in the space of time which elapses between the removal of the focusing-glass and the squeezing of the ball of the pneumatic shutter, while the focusing-screen is bent or pushed aside and the dark slide put into its place, the tap of the shutter turned off and the front of the slide drawn, the sitter is rapidly freezing, and will require bringing to life again before the exposure can be made", also from the previous feature.

One story about Sutcliffe which gives an indication of his retiring nature is on the occasion when Hadley, a well known pictorial photographer of that period, was coming from the picturesque east side of Old Whitby across the bridge spanning the River Esk and happened to meet a tall thin man carrying photographic gear. Wishing to be helpful to a brother photographer Hadley said "There's nothing worth doing over there; I've just been". The tall, thin one answered "Oh, thank you very much", turned around and abandoned the work he had set out to do.

Later the same day Mr Hadley of Nottingham called in at Sutcliffe's studio on the west side of the town and was taken aback to find that the person to whom he had given the well-meaning advice was Sutcliffe himself.

It is to a third selection of work by this early master of photography that we now welcome you. The compilation and arrangement of this book has been carried out by my son Michael who has become a partner in the gallery since the publication of the first selection. In this he has been ably backed up by my wife Dorothy, daughter Elizabeth and the gallery staff.

Bill Eglon Shaw
The Sutcliffe Gallery, Whitby
September 1990

"The Flag of Distress"

When all the power that a ship's master had at his command was the wind, shipwrecks such as this were commonplace along the North East coast. A vessel would be driven by the wind into one of the many bays with little hope of beating a course for the open sea.

The brig 'Mary & Agnes' of 174 tons, was bound for Newcastle from London with a cargo of scrap iron on 24th October 1885 when she was caught in a north-easterly gale off the coast between Sandsend and Whitby.

In an article in 'The Amateur Photographer' magazine of 14th May 1903 Frank Sutcliffe described the conditions under which this photograph was taken. "The wind was so strong that it was impossible to walk: all one could do was to crawl along on all fours; in this case a heavy camera stand shook like an aspen, a focusing cloth was an absurdity. If it had not been for the help of a big heavy soldier, an artillery man, who was on the beach at the time, who curled himself up under the tripod and held on with both hands to the two legs which caught the most wind, it would have been impossible to have done anything."   10-29

"Through the Station Doorway" − Taken on 19th September 1895. Whitby Dock End in the upper harbour, framed by the entrance to the North Eastern Railway Company's town station with the 'Friendship' boathouse in the background.   28-12

Whitby Upper Harbour, near Tin Ghaut. Taken 'against the light' from the swing bridge.   A-8

A Whitby 'cat' aground near Belle Island in the upper harbour. A 'cat' was a boat with a flat keel designed for loading and unloading cargo, very often of coal, from a beach.   7-9

"A Misty Morning"

Taken in Whitby Upper Harbour. The Penzance fishing fleet was a familiar sight in Whitby harbour on its annual visits up until the first World War.

Three of the luggers are shown here in the right foreground, where they form a subtle balance with the very delicately depicted group in the distance towards the left. It is interesting to note how this group forms an almost perfect composition in its own right. Sutcliffe realised this and a fine print of the grouping from The Royal Photographic Society's collection was reproduced in the Centenary issue of The British Journal of Photography in 1964.   E-9.

This is a 'photographer's photograph' — a man carrying a sack of coal from a collier brig into a Whitby warehouse. The extremes of lighting have been skilfully dealt with.   19-34

A snow covered wooden quayside with a barquentine and other boats laid up during winter in the Upper Harbour.   D-13

An exposure taken against the light in Whitby Upper Harbour of two boats with bare yard-arms. It bears some similarity to a painting of the same view by Atkinson Grimshaw.   4-21

The Penzance fishing fleet heads seawards down the harbour. Oars are being used to make up for the lack of wind.   3-75

The Upper Harbour with numerous boats, including cobles and brigs, near the Dock End. The picture portrays a scene of inactivity totally devoid of humanity.   26-11

The 'Rachel Lotinga', a variant of the brig-rigged sailing ship known as a 'snow', around on Whitby's harbour bar. With a displacement of 242 tons, she was built in Sunderland in 1855 and registered at Whitby in October 1874.   10-45

A Berwick registered boat in the Upper Harbour. The high peaked lugsail, mast stepped right forward and outrigger boom aft identifies her as a herring drifter.   16-46

Two Scottish 'fifies', registered at Montrose and Peterhead, moored against the New Quay in Whitby Upper Harbour.   17-29

'Cud' Colley, who appears on a number of other photographs by Frank Sutcliffe, seen standing on the 'Little Sands' at Coffee House Corner in Whitby Lower Harbour. The boats beached on the sands are cobles, typical of the North East coast and are of an ancient and traditional design dating from Viking days. Powered by sail or oars during Sutcliffe's time, they are now equipped with inboard diesel engines.   7-44

Whitby's rowing lifeboat 'Robert and Mary Ellis' being launched from the beach surrounded by crew members, many of whom are wearing cork life jackets.   31-12

The Russian schooner 'Dmitry' of Narva beached on Tate Hill sands during October 1885. Dracula is said to have arrived at Whitby in the Russian boat 'Demeter' of Varna. Did Bram Stoker derive inspiration from this subject?   3-88

Four fishermen mending nets on Whitby's East Pier with St.Mary's Parish Church on the horizon.   24-6

A clinker built coble, with its twin keel and flat bottomed stern, beached on The 'Little Sands' in the Lower Harbour. Its much deeper bow and flexible hull made it very seaworthy.   17-25

These women are gathering 'flithers' — mussels to be used as bait on their menfolk's fishing lines — on the beach at Robin Hood's Bay.   3-83

A complex yet satisfying grouping of five old fishermen taken at Staithes.   20-20

It is debatable whether Nell 'Baccus' (or Bakehouse), the girl on the right adds to the overall design of this grouping. The composition is surprisingly complete without her.

Sutcliffe exploited the mixture of smoke from fishermen's cottages and sea-fret which so often veiled Whitby. All detail was subdued and a luminous backdrop was provided for his subjects. This group of five fishergirls is very posed and yet beautifully arranged. The girl in the centre is Charlotte Constable with possibly Elizabeth Leng on her right.   16-29

A studio portrait of Anna Mary Middlemass, the daughter of a Whitby fishing family. This is an unpretentious photograph with straightforward lighting admirably suiting the subject.   A-17

One of the more obviously posed photographs. This young fishergirl is on the Scaur, near Whitby's East Cliff. The Scaur is formed of flat beds of alum shale in which fossilised marine creatures such as ammonites are often found. 18-37

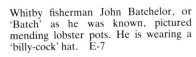

Whitby fisherman John Batchelor, or 'Batch' as he was known, pictured mending lobster pots. He is wearing a 'billy-cock' hat. E-7

Nell Bakehouse (or, colloquially, 'Baccus') at the right of this small group taken near the entrance to a Whitby yard. Both she, and John Batchelor in the photograph above right, appear on a number of Sutcliffe's photographs. A-19

The fisherlad is on top of a capstan, a wooden structure which was used to haul in be-calmed vessels which were too large to be rowed up the harbour.   12-13

"Saturday Afternoon" — The fisherman carrying a plaice by the gills was called Coulson. Plaice is a variety of flat-fish often landed at Whitby.   24-49

"Fog Bound Fishermen" — The east side of the harbour is transformed into a grey simplicity casting the six fishermen into strong relief. A print by Frank Sutcliffe was auctioned at Sotheby's during the early 1980s for £2,200.   24-15

"Fetching in the Lines" — The fishergirl holding the 'long line' is Lizzie Alice Hawksfield. The girls and fishermen's wives collected the mussels which were used as bait, often walking to beaches up to six miles away to do so.   D-49

A studio portrait of 'Tarry' Wilson. Sutcliffe's approach to studio portraiture was essentially one of great simplicity, shunning the elaborate settings used by many of his contemporaries.   30-4

An open-air fish auction at Coffee House Corner. The viewpoint is The Neptune Inn in Haggersgate. Sutcliffe used the harbour rail, visible in the mid-distance, as a setting for a number of his genre groups. In the hazy background is the East Cliff with St. Mary's church on the horizon.   2-78

Whitby Market Place in 1884 with the Old Town Hall in the background. John Stephenson or 'John the Bellman', collected rents on behalf of The Lord of The Manor. Tenants paid from 1/6d to 2/- per day for the stalls. In the late 1980s the Market Square was re-cobbled, part of a general refurbishment scheme of the east side of Whitby.   B-14

During Sutcliffe's time the building portrayed in this photograph was known as The Whitby Saloon, but later as The Spa. In 1990 work was completed on a partial restoration. 15-26

Thought to be taken at the bottom of Loggerhead Yard, off Baxtergate. This type of business was colloquially known as a 'tagereen' shop. 20-21

The interior of William Wright's Jet Workshop in Haggersgate, Whitby. It was claimed to be the only one of its kind with gas-engine powered lathes. The young boy in the foreground is George Arthur Headlam. Jet became popular during Queen Victoria's period of mourning for her husband Prince Albert, following his death in 1861, during which time she wore jewellery made from this hard, black lignite. 27-38

The Abbey of St. Hilda, Whitby, given an air of mystery by the atmospheric conditions under which this photograph was taken. 6-94

This group was taken at the foot of the 199 Steps leading up to St. Mary's Church and St. Hilda's Abbey. It is perhaps unfortunate that the iron railing partially masks the young girl's face. 19-33

Boulby Bank, off Church Street. Being built on a steep slope, the houses had balconies which allowed easy access to the upper levels. Weekly rent at the turn of the century was around 1s 3d. (Just over 6p).   13-48

Barry's Square, a short yard opening off The Cragg, an area now largely demolished, but which during Sutcliffe's time housed much of the fishing community. The cottages were built on bed-rock close into the cliff side.   A-36

Whitby under snow from the East Cliff. Taken from above Henrietta Street with St. Mary's Church at the left. Unusually, there is a good covering of snow on Tate Hill Sands near the harbourside. Normally this would have been quickly thawed by the salt-laden air.

The first documented record of the church is found in a charter of Earl Alan de Percy which dates from about 1120 A.D.

The interior of the Church is particularly interesting in having a triple decker pulpit and public galleries which were accessed by an outside staircase.

Much of the novel 'Dracula' is centred on the happenings around this church and churchyard. Bram Stoker, the book's author, visited Whitby on a number of occasions between 1885 and 1890, around the time that Frank Sutcliffe would have taken this photograph. B-7

A very atmospheric view along Pier Road, Whitby, looking south in the direction of the old swing bridge, visible at the extreme left.

Partly masking the bridge is the paddle steamer 'Flying Spray', a tug from Glasgow (GW172) which was also used as an East Coast trawler.

The Marine Hotel, Haggersgate and Coffee House Corner form a backdrop to this photograph.   11-34

Building the extension to Whitby's East Pier. This was completed in 1912 and the overhead conveyor towards the left of the picture was popularly known as 'The Iron Man'. The older, stone-built pier built during the eighteenth century is just off-camera to the right. The construction of the extension lengthened it by approximately 500 feet.   3-76

Building the railway viaduct over the River Esk. This line connected Whitby to Scarborough, with work starting in October 1882 and the first train (a locomotive and two trucks) crossing it on Friday, 24th October 1884. It has a length of over 900 feet, a height of approximately 125 feet and cost nearly £40,000, using around five million bricks in its construction.   28-11

Taken from the opposite side of the river Esk to the above photograph. The demolition of this viaduct was threatened in 1989 and if ever carried out would involve the removal of around 25,000 tons of brickwork.   27-1

The construction of Kettleness tunnel on the coastal railway line from Whitby to Loftus. This line was opened on 3rd December 1883 and was later connected with Saltburn and Middlesbrough.

The building of the tunnel became necessary due to cliff erosion and this shows the entrance on the cliff edge, at its eastern end.   27-7

During the last century milk was delivered from door to door, frequently using donkeys as a means of transport. This photograph was taken outside what was then the Abbey Inn at the top of Flowergate, a couple of hundred yards from where The Sutcliffe Gallery is now sited.

The mounting block, to assist the less agile horse rider, is still in existence, albeit in a more worn condition! B-45

The three boys are in a 'bathing machine'. These were designed to satisfy the Victorian proprieties and were drawn down to the water's edge by horses allowing bathers to step modestly into the sea, thus not exposing too much of themselves to the public gaze.

The woman with the proprietorial stance could well be the owner. 18-21

"The Bridestones" – to be found north of Staindale above Dovedale Griff. These were formed over aeons of time by the calcareous content of the landscape being eroded, leaving the stone consisting mainly of grit standing proud.

The four smartly attired gentlemen contrast strongly with Sutcliffe's more work-a-day subjects. Unfortunately their identity has not been established. 13-3

A Lawn Tennis Tournament with a bowler hatted linesman in the foreground. This is evidently a men's double match. This area has now developed into a leisure area with swimming, rifle shooting, hard-court tennis, bowling and miniature golf.

According to the Reverend George Young in his book 'A History of Whitby' published in 1817, The Union Mill Society — whose mill can be seen in the background — was founded in 1800 with around 900 members, each of whom obtained their flour at a reduced price. The principal objective was to 'furnish good and cheap flour for the use of a great part of the inhabitants of Whitby'.   30-11

Four cobles on a very calm sea in Runswick Bay. From studying the map it appears that this was taken from Cobble Dump looking in a south easterly direction towrds Kettleness.

Sutcliffe's genius for seeing the potential in the relatively mundane, shows itself in this masterpiece of beautiful tranquillity.

Writing in the Amateur Photographer magazine of 8th November 1889 Sutcliffe says "The long and the short of natural photography is that everyone sees differently, so some like to make their photographs sharp everywhere, others just the opposite.

Living in this age of freedom, I do not consider myself bound to any rules, but free to take a subject that pleases me, either as it appears in the twinkling of an eye, or as it looks after a lengthened inspection .... I find myself continually half closing my eyes, and so see less clearly than ever." C-16

Runswick Village and Bay from the south. A peaceful scene with a very calm sea on which three cobles are moored. On the beach an artist is painting beneath a parasol.   8-29

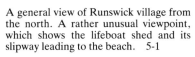

A general view of Runswick village from the north. A rather unusual viewpoint, which shows the lifeboat shed and its slipway leading to the beach.   5-1

A lone little boy leaning against a huge rock on Runswick beach. This photograph shows a thatcher (hardly visible without a magnifier) at work on the roof of the cottage at the right. He could have been starting work on the renovations resulting in the cottage's much smarter appearance in the top photograph.   5-28

Three cobles drawn up above Wayfoot at Robin Hood's Bay with a covered wagon in the background.   B-27

The three photographs on this page were taken at Robin Hood's Bay, a coastal village nestling into the cliff side six miles south east of Whitby. During Sutcliffe's time it was an active fishing community but it now caters more for the holiday maker. This view is taken looking up Bay Bank.   11-44

The village from the south with the Landing Scar exposed by the low tide. The seven cobles which can be seen hauled up the cliff side were licensed for salmon fishing — hence the 'SF' registration numbers.   4-6

Robin Hood's Bay village and Wayfoot from the East Scar. A crowd, dressed in their 'Sunday best' of men, women and children appear to have just arrived at the foot of the slip-way, probably on some kind of outing. This would be a relatively rare event and one wonders whether Sutcliffe's intention was to record them rather than the village.   11-42

Saltburn, a small coastal town nineteen miles from Whitby. Taken from near where the Ship Inn now is with Huntcliff appearing in the background. From remains found locally, it seems that Saltburn was at one time an Anglo-Saxon settlement.

In his book 'Early Man in North East Yorkshire', Frank Elgee mentions a prehistoric trackway leading from Huntcliff via Stanghow, Castleton, Castleton Ridge and over the moors to the foot of the Tabular Hills near Lastingham, a distance of twenty miles. This followed the site of barrows, or ancient burial sites established by the Urn People (roughly 400 − 1400 B.C.).

The building at the extreme right bears the inscription 'Mortuary'. This is the only photograph of Saltburn in the collection and was evidently at the geographic limit of Frank Sutcliffe's photographic territory.   26-36

This page is devoted to the small village of Sandsend, along the coast from Whitby towards the north west. The name is a literal one – the superb sandy beach extends the three miles from Whitby and ends where the cliffs of Sandsend Ness jut out into the sea.

A view along The Promenade, towards the George & Dragon Inn.   E-15

The smoke curling gently from cottage chimneys combines with moisture in the atmosphere to create a luminous haze alongside the quietly flowing Sandsend Beck imparting a rural serenity to this view.   9-5

East Row, with the beck of the same name in the mid-distance. The iron railway bridge at the left, demolished in the 1950s, carried the Whitby to Stockton line.

This photograph was taken from close to the site of the alum works, established there in 1615 by the Duke of Buckingham. Because of its proximity to the plant, East Row was built to house the workers. Alum continued to be produced until 1870.   9-15

A group of fisherpeople at Cowbar Bridge, which spanned Staithes Beck. This photograph derives much of its appeal from the crisp edge-lighting given by the afternoon winter sun.

The iron railway bridge visible in the distance was demolished in the 1950s but at this time would have carried the Whitby to Stockton line.   9-49

A view of The Staith with a row of cobles drawn up on the beach. They are all Whitby registered. 'Hard Struggle', the third cottage from the left, was constructed of stone and other materials picked up from various sources.   9-50

The village from Cowbar Bank looking seawards. The cliffs of Cowbar Nab to the west and Penny Nab to the east afford the harbour a natural protection.

The local folk-lore built up over the centuries may seem strange to 'civilized' in-comers but Shaw Jeffrey in his book 'Whitby Lore and Legend' lists many strange beliefs, probably the best known of which is the ill-luck supposed to be brought by the pig. Any mention of this animal prior to a day's fishing would lead to an immediate cancellation of the trip.   2-65

The historic fishing village of Staithes forms the subject on these two pages.

A group at the top of the slipway near The Cod and Lobster Inn, with a stack of lobster pots against the wall. The old lady is Mrs Margaret Shordon and the youngest of the boys is her grandson Robert Henry Ward, then aged three years.

Although not now such a busy fishing port, at that time practically the whole of the population relied on the fishing industry for its livelihood and towards the end of the last century forty-two cobles and fourteen larger smacks fished out of Staithes.

This is one of the latest photographs in the Sutcliffe collection, being taken around 1912.   19-28

Beggars Bridge, Glaisdale under snow with the figure of a cloaked woman.

George Harland in his book "Queen of the Dales" says that although the story leading to the construction of the bridge is often put forward as a legend there are too many facts to prove this otherwise.

The story goes that Tom Ferris, a poor boy and son of an Egton farmer, was courting Agnes Richardson, much to the disapproval of her father, the squire of Glaisdale.

Tom decided to go to sea and enlisted on a ship leaving Whitby to join the fleet which was to confront the Armada. The night before the vessel sailed he went to Glaisdale to say goodbye to Agnes. He found the Esk in flood and as there was no bridge spanning the river had to leave without seeing her. Being very disappointed he made a vow that if ever he became rich he would build a bridge over the Esk.

As well as fighting the Spaniards, he did some buccaneering and eventually returned, a wealthy man, to marry his Agnes. He built Beggar's Bridge in 1619 twelve years before his death. In his will he left the minister of Glaisdale £6 13s 4d per annum and to the upkeep of the church £2 per annum. In 1630 this was a large amount of money and as late as 1970 according to Harland, this was still being paid.   17-8

Taken at the junction of Lealholm Bank and Waupley Walls, about ten miles up the Esk Valley from Whitby. John Raw Readman of Oakley side is the waggoner and the boy standing by with the 'scuttle' over his head is Jack Frankland. Frank Sutcliffe spent much time in the Lealholm area and many of his best rural photographs were taken along Lealholmside. D-32

A general view of Goathland, a moorland village with associations extending from the burial sites of the Bronze Age (known as howes) through to the Fylingdales Early Warning Station, some three miles distant. St. Mary's Church, built in 1896, was the third to be raised on this site. The stone enclosure in the foreground is a sheep fold. Much of the local economy prior to the developing tourist industry was dependent upon sheep farming. D-7

Egton Bridge, a village eight miles from Whitby, with St. Hedda's Roman Catholic Church in the background. This church was dedicated to a former Bishop of Winchester and monk of St. Hilda's Abbey, Whitby. Sutcliffe's use of back-lighting, whilst commonplace today, was considered to be an advanced technique in the last century. C-26

Horace and Irene, two of Sutcliffe's children, at the side of a pond thought to have been behind Lodge Farm, Glaisdale. Taken circa 1889.   20-31

tled 'Peace', this fine portrait of an old
ly darning a stocking, is of Mrs Ann
arth seated in the doorway of her
me. It, together with the others on this
ge, were taken at Rock Head Cottage,
aisdale.   24-8

Mrs Scarth standing in her cottage
doorway holding a 'balm jar' containing a
'mother' culture of yeast which was
placed in the sun making available a more
or less continuous supply for bread
making. The bonnet which she is wearing
on this and the other photographs was of
a type traditionally worn by women in
both fishing and farming communities.
They had subtly differing designs
according to locality. The Staithes bonnet
is probably the best known of these and is
still occasionally worn to this day.   20-50

Ann and her husband Isaac. Grown
without any chemical 'aids', the cabbage
which Mrs Scarth is holding has already
provided a good meal for caterpillars!
Synthetic pesticides had not arrived, but
then neither had biological controls.
Today it might be called 'organically
grown' — then it was the order of the day.
Isaac, who is reading the Whitby Gazette
— founded in 1854 — was perhaps a
sufferer from gout and to give a little
more comofort appears to have split his
boots intentionally.   B-36

A charming photograph of two of Sutcliffe's daughters, Evelyn Louise, pet-named 'Lulu' with her older sister Kathy standing beside her. Taken circa 1889 at Hart Hall, Glaisdale.   13-17

"The Rake's Progress" — George Rogers (1868-1940), a shepherd of Lealholm, standing outside a stable door with Alice Chambers, a servant girl at Low Gill Beck Farm, Glaisdale. Alice is carrying a gathering rake on her shoulder. Taken in 1886.   31-14

George Scarth with his wife Ann standing on 'Long Steps' at Glaisdale. He is holding a scythe or 'lye' whilst lighting his pipe. For many years he, together with his brother Isaac, carried on business at Rock Head Cottage as a besom and scuttle maker.

To make the arduous task of mowing corn and hay easier the scythe needed to be kept razor sharp using a 'strickle'. This was a square sectioned piece of wood which was coated with grease then dipped in fine sand. The blade was then sharpened, or 'whetted' to the necessary degree of sharpness with the 'strickle' which can be seen in this photograph attached to the top of the scythe handle.   20-48

The postman-like figure seated near the water trough on Lealholm Bank was Willie Wedgewood who was born at a cottage between Houlsyke and Lealholm in 1837. He was known as the "Lealholm Express" and had a passion for uniforms — the more gold braid the better — hence the postal appearance! He died in Whitby Workhouse in 1895.   20-10

A blacksmith, John Rodgers, of Ingleneuk, Lealholmside shoeing a horse at Lealholm Hall Farm whilst Willie Wren looks on. Besides shoeing horses, a blacksmith's shop was the equivalent of our local garage, responsible for keeping things 'on the move' and the iron hoops seen here were heated and shrunk onto the wooden wheels of carts and wagons.   5-5

A back-lit group of sheep and lambs in a field between Ewe Cote Hall and the coast. It appears that Sutcliffe may have been commissioned to take this photograph as it is one of a number at the same location. This one has the most pleasing composition of the series. 24-10

Eight geese at the side of a beck. All the photographs on this page are published here for the first time and show some of the more unusual facets of Sutcliffe's photography.   14-44

A sow with seven of her piglets against the 'herring-bone' dressed wall of a farm building. This method of finishing stone is typical of much local masonry although this example is so heavily weathered that the pattern is not very evident.   15-12

Kathy Sutcliffe and sister Evelyn pose for their father on a wooden bridge, possibly in Mulgrave Woods, a few miles from Whitby. Taken around 1881. The original negative is exceptionally sharp.   9-28

A hayfield scene at Hall Park Farm, Glaisdale. The hilly terrain in this area dictated that a three-horse team was necessary to pull the wagon. The second man from the left was Tailor Bill Readman.   20-22

Rigg Mill, about three miles north west of Robin Hood's Bay. The flour mill, either water or wind powered, was an important part of the local economy before the advent of easy road and rail communication.   14-17

The south side of Egton Bridge village. The site of the cottage in which the Catholic priest Father Nicholas Postgate was born is close to the camera viewpoint. He was martyred in York in 1679.   C-2

Crunkley Gill, a delightful stretch of the River Esk between Lealholm and Danby. The angular basaltic rocks in the river are of whinstone, much used at that time for road-making.   2-95

A harvest field at Lealholm Hall Farm with 'drinkings' in progress. George Readman is on the seat of the 'rat-trap' reaper which is drawn by a two horse team.   5-4

Rowing-up potatoes with a North Cave plough in Foulbriggs Field, Lealholm Hall Farm.   11-11

A couple walking through a meadow at Factory Fields, High Stakesby, Whitby. The whole of the background to this photograph is now occupied by housing estates.   16-43

Childhood Days — Eliza, Frank Sutcliffe's wife with daughters Kathy, Evelyn and Irene. Zoe is being held in the 'scuttle'. Taken in 1889.   30-19

"Dinner Time" — One of Sutcliffe's exemplary compositions. Lealholm Hall Farm was the setting for many of Frank Sutcliffe's rural photographs. This one was taken in Foulbriggs Field and depicts two farm workers, one of whom is looking at his watch. The North Cave plough, here drawn by a two-horse team, originated at North Cave in the East Riding but this one was probably manufactured locally. The composition is faultless with a fine spatial effect being given by the back lighting and slightly hazy atmosphere, once more illustrating Sutcliffe's mastery of his chosen medium.   17-44

The man carrying a scythe and talking to a young boy in this corn field along Lealholmside is thought to have been George Readman of Lealholm Hall. Although erecting them caused hands and wrists to end up chafed, there is something far more aesthetically pleasing in these stooks than mechanically created bales, their modern equivalent.

It was in the field below this one that a U.S.A.F. F4C Phantom jet finally crashed on Friday 28th April 1979 after bouncing four times and narrowly missing cottages and the village school where fifty five children were being taught. The pilot and his fellow crew member were highly praised for their courage in avoiding the village. Both Major Donald Schuyler and his companion, Lt. Thomas Wheeler were killed in the crash.   14-7

Titled "Quo Vadis?" by Frank Meadow Sutcliffe, Honorary Fellow of the Royal Photographic Society, this moorland signpost silhouetted against a sunset sky, forms a fitting finale to this third book of his works. Where indeed are we going? As these captions are being written the Iraqi Gulf crisis hangs in the balance. Its outcome will no doubt be history by the time you read this. Periodic political upheavals cause the threat of war to hang over us from time to time; the menace of pollution and global warming are much to the fore. Sutcliffe left us, his inheritors, these magnificent photographs. What are we bequeathing to our heirs?   32-28